Not in Vain

A Biographical and Anecdotal Account

of the Life and Work of George and Helen Hart

among the Chayahuita of Peru

Ian Smith

ISBN: 151759071X
ISBN-13: 978-1517590710

DEDICATION

Soli Deo Gloria

CONTENTS

ACKNOWLEDGMENTS

This book was compiled with the aid of several people; chief among them, the Hart Family.
Special thanks to them all for permission to describe a snapshot of their parents' lives.
Doug and Ramona consented to be interviewed and gave the honor of introduction to their father as well as editing advice;
Richard and Sara provided the photos herein and editing advice.

Special thanks also to Jim and Carole Daggett for their interview and kind hospitality
And thanks to Butch and Sandy Barkman for their interview and connections to the Harts and the Daggetts.
Thanks also to Jeannie Smith, for encouragement, time, and travel, and for teaching me how to write (and much more since I was born).
Steve and Patty Marion, thanks for constant friendship and inspiration…

Mr. Marion, this book began when you said: "I wish someone would write about this."

Thank you, reader, for reading this testimony of God's work, through a man and his family and friends, in the lives of many families and their friends. May you continue to seek first the kingdom of God and His righteousness.

IAN SMITH

1

MEMORIAL

"Assuredly, I say to you, wherever this gospel is preached in the whole world, what this woman has done will also be told as a memorial to her."
– Matthew 26:13 (NKJV)

Jesus' disciples listened to much of what He taught, and several wrote it down; some preserved stories about people Jesus met and saved. The context of the story above is taken from an event that occurs in the Gospel according to Matthew (one of Jesus' disciples) shortly before Jesus' crucifixion. A woman (identified in John as Mary, the sister of Martha and Lazarus) poured some very expensive perfume out onto Jesus' feet; He knew it was for His burial. She was not necessarily aware that Jesus would die in the next few days, but somehow, the Holy Spirit moved her and she acted in such a touching way that was honoring to Jesus, and thus to God the Father.

Two thousand years down the road, that story is told in several thousand languages throughout the world, including Shawi, or Chayahuita (as the language and the people are henceforth referred to), thanks to God's work through the lives of many, including George and Helen Hart. Their labor to translate the Scriptures into Chayahuita (a particular language group belonging to a people living in Peru) impacted thousands of people through several generations and continues to do so today.

In attempting to present snapshots of George and Helen Hart's life, I hope to present the answers to two basic questions. One is: "what was God's purpose for George and Helen Hart?" The other: "how did God fulfill that purpose in their lives?" The answers come from Scripture, from interviews conducted amongst family members and friends, and from documents written by them or related to their work.

When I met Mr. Hart in 2009, he was afflicted by Alzheimer's disease, so though he remembered many things, he could not string these memories together in a linear pattern – so much of his life and experiences came together and the disease made him unable to distinguish between some of them. I will long remember two things about him that stood out to me when I got to visit with him. One was his natural sweetness in how he allowed me, a total stranger, to enter his room and speak with him after only a brief introduction by his family. The other was something he said:

"If you had told me everything I was going to do, I would have been scared to death!"

The story of George Hart's life is not one of fear, nor is it action-packed; it is a quiet one of honor and humility – and some humor. If we knew all that God has in store for us, we would be very fearful – whether it is the fear of God's holiness (which should live in all of us) or the fear of the unknown. Jesus said, "Take courage, it is I. Don't be afraid." And through Paul, our Heavenly Father who loves us says: "Perfect love casts out fear."

I have preserved the words from recorded interviews of George Hart, his son and daughter-in-law Doug and Ramona, and friends Butch and Sandy Barkman and Jim and Carole Daggett. What follows is part of the Hart's witness of God's grace in their lives, in their friends' lives, and in the lives of those they touched. Their story is a story of the family of God – a group of people working together for the glory of God. May it be a blessing and encouragement to all who read it as you seek God's kingdom and His righteousness.

"Now, may the God who gives endurance and encouragement give you a spirit of unity among yourselves as your follow Christ Jesus, so that, with one heart and mouth you may glorify the God and Father of our Lord Jesus Christ." – Romans 15:5-6 (NIV)

IAN SMITH

2

SEND ME

"Here am I. Send me!"

– Isaiah 6:8 (NIV)

I remember when the ice would be, oh, an inch thick on

the [inside of] the windows! [We would take a soapstone],

a big flat stone, and we'd heat it up on the stove, and then

put it in bed. And we would wait out in the warm part [of

the house] for the beds to heat up and so forth and then

we'd go in and take the big stones out and put 'em on the

floor somewhere else. Then we would crawl into a nice

warm bed! [We wrapped them up in] flour sacks and

newspapers… and they would cool off during the night.

And in the middle of the night, you'd wake up because

your feet had gotten onto one of the cold stones, and we

would kick it out of bed! We also slept in long-johns and

heavy clothes with lots of blankets and quilts….

In the summer, we'd just open the windows.

Oh, yah, it got hot…. But compared to Peru, it was nice and cool![1]

George

George Elton Hart was born on Flag Day, June 14, 1922, in the farming community of Stanton, Michigan, to George and Ellen Hart. George's father worked as a mail carrier for many years, thus he was able to support his family through the years of the Great Depression. During those years, George attended school, worked the farm, and participated in

[1]Hart, Doug; (2009); Dad Memories 4; sound file on disc "George Hart"; files copied to disc 11/29/09.

local sports: basketball, track and field competitions, and football. His

siblings often attended these games, but his parents seldom did. His

mother would often inquire as to how one event or another went, but it was

mostly out of love for her son rather than interest in the sport itself.

George was the fifth of seven children: Lola (born to George's

father's first wife before she died), Charles B., Gerald Thayer, Wilma,

himself, Raymond and Arlene (adopted into the family).

> We had several cows and a couple of horses.... In the
>
> middle of the week we had prayer meetings. Sunday
>
> morning, we went to church; Sunday night too. I
>
> remember when dad used a horse on the mail route,
>
> especially in the wintertime.
>
> That was just life in those days![2]

---

[2] Hart, Doug; (2009); Dad Memories 4; sound file on disc "George Hart"; files copied to disc 11/29/09.

George and Parents

Not long after he completed high school, war broke out in Europe and in the Pacific. Many young men volunteered or were drafted into the American armed forces to combat the rise of the Axis powers, and George was one of those. His athleticism and dedication to his studies prepared him for the new, technical, and dangerous experiences he would encounter. In an interview with his son, Doug, he recalls his reasons for joining the Army Air Force and some of the events that followed his decision:

And then the war started and was on, and some of my buddies… in fact, there were three of the fellows I had played football and basketball and track and so forth with, they were killed in New Guinea before I ever went into the Army.

And I didn't want to get into the Army, and I said, 'Well, I've never been up in an airplane! I'd like to be a pilot.'

So, I signed up and took the exam…. Everybody was going to sign up. In those days, everybody signed up and if you didn't, they took you! Thayer never went because he had a bad knee, and a soldier that's got a bad knee isn't much good. [Charlie] was older at the time, and he never got drafted.

I'd rather be a pilot than a foot soldier, [so I went] down to Grand Rapids, I took the exam and I passed it. I got in and I just waited. And between the time that I signed in and so forth, my buddies who were down in the Reserves were killed in New Guinea.

I took the pilot training and started out – the way they did the process at the time – to train to be a pilot. Every branch of the service had a basic training… it's usually the hardest time getting adjusted. Before, I'd never seen the ocean. I remember, it was in the middle of the winter when I got the notice to depart for Detroit. My dad took me down – it was fifteen degrees below zero – to Detroit. And three days on the troop train, and our base was the twentieth story of a luxury hotel – a high rise. And I had left all my stuff on the beach; I had never been to the ocean! It was the middle of January.

I stayed there – they didn't have room in the flying school – they had a training program, where you learned to adjust to the airplane, and so forth, and took classes, and so forth. I went back up to Ohio, it was early spring, and we were there for about four months, beautiful time of the year. And then, in the middle of June, they called us down to flight school in Texas. And I did that way into the Fall, before we moved to – it's between Dallas and Forth Worth – primary flight school. I was at flight school all

Fall and through the Winter, and I graduated that in April.

And then we got our wings, and then we went to the

preparation for where we did our C-47 training. They gave

you a chance to say what you wanted. I asked for a

medium-sized bomber, and I thought that's what I was

getting into. And they put me in a C-47 to be a troop

carrier. And I had all my training in that and the European

war was still going on, so they trained us for the European

theatre, and we had towing gliders and all that kind of

thing that never took place! And after all of that, I got put

in a troop carrier and was sent to India!

IAN SMITH

3

PLANS

"For I know the plans I have for you, declares the Lord, plans to prosper you and not to harm you, to give you a hope and a future."

– Jeremiah 29:11 (NIV)

The war years were some of the best and worst years of George Hart's life. Like most of the young men who enlisted or were caught up in the draft, he had little idea what was in store for him. The military trained George in the skill of flying, a skill quickly transformed into art – the aerial ballet that is the mass transportation of supplies over long distances and treacherous terrain. As a copilot, he flew the C-46 and later the C-47 – a juggernaut of an aircraft with a tremendous wingspan and a large cargo-hold. Those who flew in one remember well the feelings they had as they watched the wingtips bounce up and down, almost flapping, as the ship tried to get airborne! For a while, his unit was stationed in Burma, supporting the Chinese soldiers as they strove to drive the Japanese out.

Later, they shifted northwards where George became one of the few courageous men to fly "the Hump."

"The Hump" was a supply route designed to keep the transport aircraft safe from enemy fighters. Since the Japanese controlled a good deal of airspace, that meant flying over the dangerous Himalayan Mountains. Each mountain has its own weather system; that makes flying over or around them tricky at best, even with advances in technology seventy years later. In the forties, navigational systems consisted of triangulation using radio frequencies as well as compasses. Pilots had to trust their navigators with their lives as much as navigators trusted the pilots to keep the craft in the air.

This trust played a major role in one anecdote George shared with his family many years after the war ended. He recalled one evening when all his fellow soldiers were out at a local bar carousing the night before a scheduled flight. George was the only one who did not go with them. He stayed at the barracks and read his Bible. He knew they were out there somewhere in the night, having fun and growing their friendships with one another, and he felt like he should have been there with them – except that he did not share their enthusiasm for drink. "That was the loneliest I've ever been," said George.

However, he grew closer to God while maintaining his integrity, and the Lord rewarded him for it the next day. His group was scheduled to fly some cargo from one point to another; a fairly routine mission, only the pilot and several other crewmembers had nasty hangovers from the night before. The takeoff was alright, and so the majority of the flight. Then it came time to land. The pilot looked over at George and said, "Would you take this one? I'm not feeling so great."

George took the controls and guided the giant flying machine safely onto the ground. God's gentle training in George's life provided a way for common grace to touch the lives of the men on that plane, if only for a moment. For, without George remaining faithful to his convictions about what was right and wrong – what honored God and what glorified oneself – it is likely that things could have gone very wrong for those men that day.

George in the Army

After the war, George caught a ride home on a troop ship where he met a couple of gentlemen with similar beliefs and values. They told him about their plans to go to Wheaton College, and so he decided he would go there too.

George met his wife-to-be Helen while he was preparing to translate God's Word into other languages. Their son Doug and his wife Ramona remember George's love for the Bible and his love for his wife:

Doug:

I know he loved the Psalms and he loved Proverbs. He told me he would include the reading of one Proverb each day during his devotions. So he'd pick the day of the month – that Proverb. I don't remember specific verses. I do remember there was a verse that he picked to be part of the memorial service for my mother when she died – I actually bookmarked it in my Bible reader here: Psalm 73:23. There's a segment that he left out: "Yet I am always with You; You hold me by my right hand. You guide me with your council and afterwards, You will take me into glory. Who have I in heaven but You, and earth has nothing I desire besides you. My flesh and my heart may fail, but God is my strength and my portion forever."

And in verse 28: "As for me, I have made God my refuge. I will tell of all Your deeds." And to him, that captured my mother and her love for the Chayahuita people and her love for serving God. In many ways, you can't talk about them separately. They were married for 50 years and their entire ministry to the Lord was together.

Ramona:

I don't know the reference for this, if it comes from
Proverbs; Dad was telling it to me to learn, was the verse
that talks about "Better a patient man than one who can
take over a city." And he was a very, very patient person.

George's patience is evident in the way he conducted himself in
preparation to learn how to translate Scripture. In an interview with his
son, George recalls many of his experiences in those years leading up to his
travels to Peru.

I was a Bible major. And I couldn't go into fly – you had
to have your mechanic's license, and I had had no
background in that whatsoever. So that would have taken
a lot of months and years to get that. But, by that time, I
was interested in missions – foreign missions.

Here's where I got acquainted with Jim Elliot, Ed McCully,
and Nate Saint. We were in a fellowship group together
and we would meet together in prayer.

He was in prayer all the time.

Jim Elliot was really a general leader of the Christian work
while we were there. I knew three of them well. Ed
…went to Harvard… and was on the track team. Nate
Saint was a pilot. He was the one who initiated the act
where you circle around [a potential landing site and lower
something down to the people below with a long rope].
Bill Godsworth was the coach. He would get these letters
from these old ladies that would quote the Psalms, "Glory
not in the works of thine own hands…" And they would
sort of run him down. But they didn't know what he was
talking about: the legs of a man was a soldier's best
weapon. Nobody could be a soldier in the army in those
days – and what it was talking about was not depending
upon the soldiers.

4

SMALL THINGS

"For who has despised the day of small things?"

– Zechariah 4:10

College was another proving ground for George. It did not matter what he was doing; he could see the hand of God in many ways. There were many activities he participated in that God used to prepare him for work in the mission field later in life. One of these areas is athletics. Even on the mission field, George continued to play various sports and maintained his level of fitness so that he could traverse the jungle. Another area was his training in understanding God's Word. He recalls some of his college experience.

> You know what was one of the most dangerous sports in college? Pole vaulting! I did the hurtles some in college, but I had to switch feet on every other hurtle. I ran a couple of the relays – hurtle relays. Yeah, but I wasn't really good. I had learned to run in an open field.

I took a lot of courses. In summertime, I usually went to a camp – it was a camp up in Wisconsin. I don't remember the name. One of my best buddies was Sky Johnson from Grand Rapids. He was required to do Seminary work and we went to the Japanese church. I spoke there; he was one of the missionaries. It was right about the same time that I got married.

I stayed there for two years afterwards. I got interested in translation and made my plans to go to the University of Oklahoma before I sailed. I was at Wheaton for two years … and after my degree in Bible, I went to graduate school for two years.

The best preparation for translation was the Gospel [Class]. He [my teacher] went through and explained the background, he had a tremendous background in Biblical studies, ad he explained most of the sermons … When you're talking to someone, or teaching someone, you don't tell him what he already knows, and the background of the Pharisees – what they believed and why they did – many of these things, came out of the background that they had.

The second course which I took that was extremely useful

was "The Epistles." Paul's work – and he gave the background (implicit information, we call it) – when you talk to someone, you don't tell him the stuff he already knows. ...we don't know why he said these things. For example, one of the Pharisees' laws was there were so many steps [you could take on the Sabbath]. You could walk all you wanted to on your own property, but off your own property, you could only take this many steps and beyond that, you were breaking the law – on the Sabbath. Jesus complained about their hypocrisy – well, this is one of the things I never knew about. There were so many steps you could take, so they would have a servant take some of their clothing or a robe or something and they would take it to a friend's house who they wanted to visit on the Sabbath. They would take it the day before, and leave it there, and then if I owned that, I could go over there, and I could walk as many times [steps] as I wanted to! That was all right according to their [law].... But the Bible doesn't tell you that. Jesus never mentioned these things when he was speaking to the Pharisees. But it helps to understand these Gospel stories, because these laws of prohibitions which they didn't put on their own, was totally contrary to the Law.

5

FAVOR

"He who finds a wife finds a good thing, and obtains favor from the Lord."

– Proverbs: 18:22 (NKJV)

"He who finds me [wisdom] finds life, and obtains favor from the Lord."

– Proverbs 8:35 (NKJV)

Then he met Helen.

> I knew [Helen's] sister marginally. I was in the same
> graduating [class]. I went to SIL in Oklahoma. She was a
> grammar teacher there. In a big course, at the end, you
> were assigned a language and there were all these processes
> to prepare for translation. She was in charge of that; I was
> in her group that she was in charge of. We had to work
> together and we found that we work together very, very
> well. She worked at Mexico with the Stewarts working

with the Amuzco tribe, helping them with their translation [during the summer]. It was a good two or three years she was down there – I was at Wheaton – she was four years ahead of me.

We were married and I graduated four years after her. In the fall she went to the University of Michigan to get her Masters while I was finishing grad school. I was there [Norton, Oklahoma] two summers. When she was in Michigan I corresponded with her often. I went to a Michigan football game with her. She just went there one year. Based on how bright she was, they tried their best to get her to switch her major to anthropology. But she knew they never let you get your Masters without going on to get your Doctorate. She had no interest in getting her PhD and having to go all around the world. After that, she went to CBC and taught Bible school in Grand Rapids.

Well, [jungle camp], it's a whole winter. While I was down there, she was in Michigan, and she didn't get back for the wedding until a week before. Her mother did all the planning by correspondence. She did all the planning for the wedding, because neither one of us were there until a week before the wedding!

She [Helen] went to public schools there [in Chattanooga]. She was an excellent student. She was very involved with the Christian organizations in the school. She was very active and when Mom passed away we got a card from a guy who was with her in high school. He had never forgotten her; she had so impressed him with her Christianity while in high school! He remembered her and sent condolences and wrote a letter about how much he appreciated her.

Helen

George loved his wife and learned everything he could about her and her family. God brought them together because He knew they would serve Him best working side by side. Helen loved George and worked with him for many years. He remembers the following about her and her family.

> [We were married at Westminster Presbyterian in 1955 in Chattanooga] It was a pretty good sized church. There were individual friends [who supported us in Peru].

> [Her father was well-respected.] He had the strangest work schedule of any doctor I've ever heard: he would get up…at four o'clock in the morning and went to the hospital, took care of all his patients in the hospital, had his breakfast, and started his office hours at six o'clock in the morning! And from six until ten was his part of the day. Everybody in Chattanooga knew Dr. Long. He was the first technical pediatrician – specialist – and he took care of everybody. Everybody in Chattanooga had a black waiting room and a white waiting room, and that was just the way it was. Nobody broke it. And he didn't break it either, but all the blacks – they got exactly the same care as the whites did. The only difference was the blacks paid half as much as the whites did. And he kept that up for

his whole career.

He was brought up on a farm; he loved it. So he bought this farm; it took awhile to get it started. When he first started, he didn't have a lot. He had his choice: he could buy a house for his family to live in, or he could invest money in a company that was just getting started up. He decided "what to do?" Well, he decided to put his family first. And this other little company that was just getting started that he would have had original stock in was called Coca-Cola. He would have been a millionaire! But he put his family first. He said, "I never regretted it."

…He did not work on Sundays, but he would go out on emergencies. He was an expert in diagnosis. He was known all over the south for expertise in diagnosis. After he died, somebody from Washington came out and interviewed her because he had such a reputation. Everybody in Chattanooga knew Dr. Long. We would go to a restaurant, and I remember all sorts of people coming up to talk to us. He was respected not only for his doctoral abilities, but for his Christian faith.

We got married on a Friday afternoon [June 3rd] and went to Lots Bar up there. And we spent Saturday, Sunday and Monday we had to leave to get down to the University of Oklahoma so we could both start teaching.

After we had spent the summer there [SIL] we went to the biannual conference they had in Sulphur Springs. One day, Carol Goodall – who was the Missions director for Peru – took us aside and said, "We've been trying for about five years to get somebody to take this job." So, we got our support.

Our church [Westminster] and the Japanese church and the one in Hart, Michigan [gave us support]. It was in January, I think, because we hadn't even gone out yet when we heard about the Auca incident. We were in the mission house when I heard. Mom knew Betty Elliot very well. It was a dorm house. It was a real shock to us. Mom corresponded with Betty Elliot for years.

6

PATH

"Your word is a lamp to my feet and a light to my path."

– Psalm 119:105 (NKJV)

Once they were married, George and Helen set about the task of preparing for Bible translation. These days, organizations like Wycliffe Bible Translators have very specific processes and criteria for preparing to translate the Word of God into another language. When George and Helen started, they had some framework to build upon, but they had a much steeper learning curve than they had imagined. He remembers some impressions from the early days of being in Peru.

[Yarinacocha] was small.

We were on the second row [of houses]. The first row along the lake had been pretty well taken up by the time we got there. We learned Spanish in Lima; we studied for two or three months before we went out there.

I know we had gone in January. Our experience in Lima was not a good language situation.

My wife was having a baby and was out most of the time. She kept coming up with red spots on her. We found out later that they were bed bugs! They never touched me – they didn't like my blood I guess.

There were other couples; some we hardly ever saw. One couple stayed with us. The family didn't eat until 2:30 or 3:00 o'clock in the afternoon.

Funny part about … every time I got on a bus, I got bitten with fleas – they didn't bother her at all. Between the bed bugs and the fleas…[we were both eaten up]!

Right after [the conference in the spring] we went up to Yurimaguas. And we had read in the Reader's Digest about this woman from New York City who had gone down [to Peru] and [got] married. They had a farm right in the middle of the Chayahuita territory. We wanted to see about the possibility of seeing them briefly. She had a house so big and so long, and our radio area was put up inside the room. Her husband died, and she took over the hacienda that was among the Chayahuitas. For the first few years, she was ruling the Chayahuitas – it was the remnant of the patron system from Europe. The landowners had all the land, and she had a big kitchen. One of the fellows came out and helped me clear a place for an airfield on the Paralagona River. So we stayed at her house and she had us eat with her – she had a cook.

The house had big walls were over a meter wide [adobe]and twelve foot ceilings…. We ate in the kitchen, and the kitchen didn't have a ceiling really – they had bats. Bat droppings would fall in the soup.

We [stayed there] until they got the airfield done. We got up there by boat – Ray Litke and I. [Then] we flew to Yurimaguas. We met the Chayahuitas there. As soon as we got the airfield finished, [Helen came out].

IAN SMITH

7

CHAYAHUITA

Then Jesus came to them and said, "All authority in heaven and on earth has been given to me. Therefore go and make disciples of all nations, baptizing them in the name of the Father and of the Son and of the Holy Spirit, and teaching them to obey everything I have commanded you. And surely I am with you always, to the very end of the age."

– Matthew 28:18-20 (NIV)

The Chayahuita, or Shawi, are a small ethnic group of people living in the rainforest region of Peru, not far from Yurimaguas. In the year 2000, their population was about 11,400. They are a friendly group and trade frequently up and down rivers: primarily the Ucayali and Marañon Rivers. These rivers flow down from the Andes and grow larger until they feed into the Amazon. The people there speak the language that shares their tribal title.

Chayahuita is classified as a Cahuapanan language, which is a distinct class in its own right in the world. It is not related to the Quechuan language class which has over 10 million speakers in 45 dialects living in six different countries. Quechua is the language spoken 500 and more years ago by those people called the Incas. Inca, according to scholars, is not the proper name for the people group, but rather the leader of the Quechua.

No one is yet certain where the Chayahuita language comes from. It may have roots in some early American languages, or it may come from parts of Asia or Polynesia. That is a puzzle for ethnographers and linguists to solve! One of the reasons for the survival of this language is the isolation of the people. The Chayahuita live in a densely forested region of Peru surrounded by high, rugged mountains and terrain that is navigable mostly by thin footpaths through the thick growth or by the highways of the jungle – rivers and streams. Even the Quechua people (whose carefully governed and managed empire extended across most of Peru, Chile, and Ecuador, and parts of Bolivia and Argentina) scarcely had contact with this solitary group. The imperial control of the Inca had its limitations, and he was not able to begin constructing roads that forged into the jungle as the Incan line ran out of time and power. A civil war further weakened the Inca's power when a horrid plague hit the great Quechua.

The Spanish explorers who made inroads into the western side of South America quickly overwhelmed the Inca and his people and laid low the once mighty empire through superior military tactics, bravery, cunning, and deceit. Spain then set up many colonies in this rich area which, in conjunction with her other colonies in many other parts of South and Central America, provided her coffers with much gold and other supplies for her European wars. With colonization, came subjugation, and a dramatic change in terms of language and culture. The Chayahuita managed to weather all of these storms, secluded in their quiet villages and practicing their animistic religions.

The colonial people, and those who accepted the new foreigners, quickly spread their influence deeper into the jungle. Trade began to increase, some roads (where engineers could manage to place them) were built, and traffic increased on the rivers. Spanish was now spoken widely across Peru (and many other South American countries) and Quechua began to take a back seat. With trade came missionaries; some seeking to spread the Good News that Jesus Christ, the Son of God, has come to make a way for us to be in fellowship with God – even after we sinned and disobeyed Him.

Today, 500 years after the fall of the Inca, the Chayahuita still speak their own tongue, as well as some Spanish, so that they may make trades for shotguns and machetes and other goods. Like many other small language groups around the world, Chayahuita was primarily an oral language, with no written characters to represent the sounds. Today, thanks largely to the work of George and Helen Hart, the Chayahuita have a written form of their language including a dictionary, a translated Bible, and many supporting documents explaining the language to those who will study it in the future. This means that the Chayahuita are now much more in communication with the rest of the world than they once were.

8

FAMILY

"...Fulfill my joy by being likeminded..."

– Philippians 2:2 (NKJV)

George and Helen were seldom separate from one another. I interviewed their son Doug and his wife Ramona at their home in Ohio and they remember the following about their parents and growing up in the mission field.

> Doug Hart: We'd been talking about when he was growing up, since his father's name was George, and my dad's first name was George, he was known by his middle name: Elton. That reminded me of one of my dad's jokes: one of many! When this guy went into... this guy was known by his initials only; that's what he was given: R. B. Jones. And so he wanted to make sure that the Army got that right when he enlisted. So, when he was filling out the paperwork, he put down "R" and in parenthesis, "only,"

"B" parenthesis "only" "Jones". So, naturally the Army took that, processed it, and from then on he was known as "Ronly Bonly Jones"!

Well, he was always a very active person. From his childhood, he was an athlete: he was a track star, he was a football star, he was a basketball star. Even in college, he competed at Wheaton college as an athlete in the pole vault. This was back in the days when the pole vault was done with a bamboo pole and fiberglass came along afterwards. He was a sprinter, so he did the hundred-meter/hundred-yard dash. I was born when he was in his mid thirties. I knew him at a later age when he was mid forties and above and athletics was a part of his life.

Ramona Hart: Very self-disciplined.

Doug: He would play pick up games of basketball in the late afternoon after work, and then later, after basketball, he picked up on tennis. He taught us kids to play tennis. And we would play tennis several times a week. As a family, we would play tennis when we would come up in furlough like in the summer we'd go down and play tennis every day. In addition to playing basketball, he would come home sweaty and eat supper with us – it always used to bother my sister, I believe! He would always after playing basketball, he would go for a short run before supper, so he'd come home like that.

Ramona: He liked to bike ride too. He went from running, which eventually got to his knees, to riding his bike, and he rode his bike well into his eighties.

Doug: In fact, I have his bike out in my garage.

Ramona: We had to take it away from him.

Doug: Because, when he moved into this retirement home, he wanted to be sure to bring his bike along. He had it in his mind that he was going to be living independently and that he was going to be riding his bike to stay in shape. So it's partly just a reflection of the discipline that was ingrained into him and it was a part of his life.

He liked to read; we always used to get, when we were growing up, there were two magazines that we always got, and that was the Reader's Digest and National Geographic.

Ramona: And he loved to read books by Jerry Bridges. Because, he bought some for us and got us into Jerry Bridges: <u>The Pursuit of Godliness</u>, <u>The Pursuit of Holiness</u>.

Doug: There were different authors he liked besides that: Phillip Yancey.

Ramona: He loved his book about prayer. In fact, he gave us a copy the same year we gave him one! We just kind of exchanged books!

Doug: Very much a thinker.

Ramona: He would read a little, and spend some time reflecting on that little bit he read. And he would say, "You can't read the chapter, you can't just read through the book, you have to just read the little bit and then think about that." And he would go on from there, just a little at a time, just a little at a time. And he would always share what it was that he had read and what he had learned about and what it was that God was teaching him and it always came up some time during the day.

Doug: So, we grew up at a center in the jungle near the town of Pucallpa. And there were several hundred missionaries there. Since our family, my parents were translators, we would go out to the tribe every summer and spend the entire three months – spend the summer out in the tribe as a family.

Hart Family – 1967

As a result of that, we kind of interacted some with the Indians, with the other Indian kids, and developed friendships and activities there, but you know, your culture's somewhat different too, so we developed somewhat more close-knit ties with the family, because we would do more as a family than your typical small-town or large-town and relationships that were more widespread outside the family. So a lot of my memories of my father and mother and of us kids were doing things as family. There were times when we would go into Lima for a vacation and I remember going down to the ocean and going swimming. This is the Pacific Ocean, and you have the Humboldt Current comes up along the west side of South America, and it comes from the Arctic originally, and it's warmed up some, but the water's very, very cold there. And the waves are very good there along the coast. I can remember going swimming many times in the ocean with my father and with the entire family. So, we kind of developed a love for the water and the ocean. When we were living in the states, our family likes a beach vacation, and may father would also love to play in the waves. And up until two years ago, when he was like 84 or 85, he would walk out at that age, and get in the waves. The last time we took him down there, it was hard for him to maintain his balance. We learned our love for playing in the ocean…he still loved doing that into his eighties.

Ramona: And what about camping? He taught you boys

all about camping, you boys went camping at a young age.

Doug: Yeah, we did go as a family but on the subject of camping, you have to understand the tribal situation. So what our life was like when we'd go out in the summer. The Indians live off the land. Especially at that time, they had minimal contact with the outside world. They would raise rice as a cash crop or they would hunt some animals and sell the furs. They would trade with the Peruvian community; they would trade their rice and their furs for money and would buy the minimum of supplies in the form of machetes, shotgun, shotgun shells, maybe some kerosene, pots – though they had pottery that they made as well. And then they would take those back to their villages. They lived off the land as they had done for thousands of years, built their homes from the trees, tied them together with vines, built thatched roofs for the houses. They lived on the rivers and still do. They would travel, some by trails, but a lot by dugout canoes on the rivers. So, when we traveled in the tribe, we traveled the same way. We traveled by dugout canoe, and there would be times when we'd be traveling from one village to the next and it might take several days to make that trip,

especially if the river was down.

9

WHAT TOOK YOU SO LONG?

"A cord of three stands is not quickly broken."

– Ecclesiastes 4:12

I also interviewed two friends of George and Helen: Butch and Sandy Barkman along with Steve Marion, a mutual friend of all and one of my greatest mentors. (It was he who first spoke of George Hart to me.) Butch and Sandy came from slightly different backgrounds, but the Lord brought these two together and brought their path alongside that of George and Helen in the mission field working with the Chayahuita. Here follows a bit of back-story of how God brought them all together.

> Butch Barkman: Well, at age fifteen in a Christian high-school, [I heard that] five men were killed in the jungles of Ecuador, and my concept of missions at that point was that you had to be: a doctor, pastor, teacher or nurse. And one of those guys – the fifth one I read about in our school library after their death in Life magazine – was a

47

pilot. I was a farm-boy and I understood technical things, so I just remember saying out loud: "Hey, I could do this. I could learn how to repair and drive an airplane!" And the Lord just kept that vision.

I went into the US Navy because we were not a family with a lot of finances, so I couldn't learn how to fly and go to those kinds of schools. And so I went into the Navy and got GI bill, which I used, and then I met Sandy in the Navy and I started getting my training. All of my training I got because of that GI bill.

And then we made an application. I thought I was going to join Mission Aviation Fellowship. But I had one qualification of theirs that I didn't meet. So we went across town in Southern California to the Wycliffe headquarters and they said: "Oh, we need people."

So we walked out of there with the preliminary questionnaire and three months later we were being evaluated and Nolan University campus and the rest is history. That's the short version.

There's a lot of different things that happened along the

way there – answers to prayer, and how God guided us and kept us focused. Because, I kept saying: "As long as this door is open, this is where we're going." And there kept being opportunities to go into a commercial venture somewhere. I worked part time for Ryder truck rental company while I was going to school. And they offered me a full time job – they offered me a franchise almost. And they would train me – a great company to work for. And I said, "Well, if this doesn't work out, can I come back?" And he said, "Sure." I never went back.

Who knows where I would have ended up in Ryder truck rental corporation if I had stayed there; I really enjoyed the organization – a great company.

Butch and Sandy recall the following about working with George and Helen:

Butch Barkman: George was I think on Wheaton College's tennis team when he was a student there; I know he was on the track team there as a sprinter as a young man, so he always, if he wasn't playing tennis, he was jogging or exercising. Very athletic, very conscious, very disciplined.

Sandy Barkman: I don't remember George walking anywhere! He was always fast walking or running!

Butch: Or he was on his motorcycle. He had a little Honda 90 with a little square platform on the back and he had a little dog. And that dog, when George got on his motorcycle, the dog would hop on there. And if he went around the corner too fast, the dog went flying. He would stop, the dog would jump back on and there they'd go again! So it was just George and his dog, it was so cute.

At some point, he got hit in the eye. Someone tried to slam the ball and that eye was permanently damaged so it was always dilated; so, he always had to wear dark glasses/ ' Course, in the Amazon there's always bright sunshine, and here like we've had this last week, just very, very bright sunlight. But it didn't stop him from doing his work at all. As a WWII pilot, he flew C-47 transports out of India across the Himalayas into China to feed the Chinese people. And they made a lot of friendships there. I asked him one day, I said: "How did you navigate?" He said: "Well, what we had were called automatic direction finders – ADFs. They function off of AM radio and so the signal can't always be very accurate. It would go from 90 degrees to your left to 90 degrees to your right. We would fly right in the middle of that. We always had enough altitude to fly in the Himalayas and as they'd get to China, as they got a little lower in altitude, the signal became more accurate. We only lost two airplanes all those years.

Steve Marion: The C-47s weren't pressurized, were they?

Butch: No, they weren't but the pilots had oxygen masks. They'd go to like 25,000 feet and then cross over. So the pilots were on oxygen, and you could handle that.

[A story that comes out of China is that Chinese man was helping a friend of ours meet people in different provinces in China.] They were on a train and he said to the man, "I know your culture and that someday you're going to ask me for a favor, because you've been doing me all these favors. So I'm going to owe you." And this gentleman said: "When I was a boy, these aviators would pass out food and these little candies with holes in them (we know them today as lifesavers) and we kids loved those things, and they literally saved our lives. And I said at that time, if I can ever do an American a favor, I'll do it. So this is payback to you; you don't owe me anything."

We had two Catalina flying boats for years, and we would use them to bring people like the Chayahuitas, we'd bring them in to a training course so they could learn to be teachers, bilingual teachers in their language group area. So the Catalina was used for that for like ten or twelve years. Well, George could fly one of those; in fact they put him in the left seat of one of those, which is the pilot's seat of it. And he said: "Well, guys, I've had my thrill in flying, I'm going to do Bible translation now!" So they were focused on that. That had to have been probably in the 70s.

Sandy: They came down together.

Butch: I think most of their kids were born on the furlough or in Peru. Doug is the oldest; he's an engineer in Ohio. Dick is a missionary in Bolivia. Karen is a registered nurse, and they live in Philadelphia.

I don't recall if they had major health issues, but they stuck with it. Helen was a lady, kind of nervous; afraid to fly. Which, at one point they were considering terminating our flying circuits just because it was a political issue with the government. And she said, "If our JAARS guys have to go home, I'm going right with them, because I won't fly with the local guys: they're not safe and I'm already afraid." So we tried to be very gentle with her in the plane; make gentle turns because we knew she was a very nervous lady, but very talented. I think her father was chairman of the board at Bryan College in Tennessee for many years. He was a doctor and he brought that school – there's probably some history at Bryan College about this man – from relative obscurity to being a well-known school as chairman of the board.

We were in their prayer group. In our center there in Yarinacocha, every translation team had people like Sandy and me who were called support workers, and we were on their support team not in terms of finances, but in terms of doing things for them: like praying with them once a week, finding out what their issues were, things that were happening. If there was a crisis out there in the village, a sickness, an epidemic or something, we'd get together and pray with them. We'd send them off in the airplanes, we'd bring them back, have a meal with them when they came back ('cause they didn't have any food in the house). So, we'd have them in our home and just kind of take care of them that way and try to encourage them in that sense.

Yeah, we flew out there all of the time. We had a major accident on one of the airstrips. George was in one of the airplanes: George and a doctor and another pilot. No one was injured; the pilot had a little scratch on his leg. The airplane was just about destroyed, but in that particular community, they were resisting the translation and the Gospel. And when they saw how everyone came in, they dismantled the airplane, put it in – they made two dugout canoes, and lashed them together – they put the landing gear in each canoe, and with the motor in the back, they took it downriver to the biggest town, and then they put it in Peruvian Army helicopters and brought it to Yarinacocha and we rebuilt the whole thing. But, the people saw how everybody teamed together to work, and it just suddenly made a whole difference in the way they looked at the Gospel. And today, there's a very strong church there.

Sandy: When they saw it going for the trees, they thought they would all be dead. And they saw them walking out and they couldn't believe that they would be saved!

Butch: Yep, it was a life-changing experience for them. And that village was Solidad. I've been there many times. I came in one day to make a flight, and I heard Helen who was in the outer part of the office: "Now the pilot has to give a bunch of shots on this one."

And I said: "Oops, that's me! I don't know how to give shots." So I went out and told them they had to change pilots. And they said, "Just go out to the clinic and learn."

So I went up to the clinic and they taught me – it was just DPT shots, as simple as you can get, and it was for the children. Ages about four through seven and there were about sixty-five or seventy of them. So the teacher, the bilingual teacher wrote down all their names – this was for the government – they called a name and they came over and I just kind of put them over my knee, and (little boys were mostly naked, they don't cover them up until they're about ten; little girls were mostly covered, and that's good) so little girls I'd pull their drawers down a little bit and swab the hip, and one of theirs skin was so tough, the needle just bounced off. I bent the needle on another one. One little boy was so scared, he wet right down my leg. So that was kind of unpleasant! But after that was over, we got that done OK and after that was over, they thought I was a doctor. And I said: "I just give them shots! I'm really not a doctor!"

But they had a guy and they said, "He's dying, you've got to look at him."

And I said, "OK."

So we went over there and he was lying in his hammock — he was pretty pale; I put my hand on his forehead and he didn't have a temperature. So I said, "Where do you have pain?"

He said, "In my mouth."

And I said, "Well, what caused the pain?"

And he said, "Well, I was cleaning my shotgun and it went off and kicked me right in the teeth!"

And he opened his mouth and his front two teeth were

sticking out straight. Well, we had just had an experience with our son, who was like seven or eight – nine, something like that – and he slipped on a chair and did the same thing. And a dentist just pushed them down.

And I said to this guy: "Just push your teeth down and then don't eat anything hard with those teeth, don't bite down on anything for at least a week. Let those teeth get firm again in your mouth."

I just happened to be out there again in two or three weeks, and I said, "Is your patient, is he still around?"

And there he was standing in the circle, but he hadn't eaten or had been drinking in two days. And I said, "If you don't start drinking water or whatever you drink, and eating, you're going to die!"

I was that blunt. But there he was in the circle, doing fine, so it was just great! I learned a lot. In fact there was a dentist there who taught me how to give Novocain injections. And a lot of the people have such bad teeth, you're better off to pull them. So I pulled a lot of teeth.

Well, when Mr. Hart came, they were not encouraged to

learn Spanish. They were encouraged to learn only the language of the people they were assigned to. It was about a little over an hour flight north northeast of our center. One pretty large city there with an airstrip – a commercial airstrip. Their highways were rivers or trails. Another thirty minutes or so out into the middle the language spread out into two river systems. People like you and I, Steve, [tall people] would have trouble getting through these trails: they just run right through things. So they went out and these people were monolingual. So these people had to learn by picking up an object and learning how they put sentences together. And there's a science of linguistics where you can do that very quickly. But, as far as the history of how long it took them to translate, I don't have any information on that.

George sometimes would go out by himself. Generally, when we'd go out, we'd cook over an open fire. We didn't call that camping, that was life among the Chayahuitas. At some point, when they begin to accept the Gospel, they begin to name their villages [for example] Nuevo Luz – which is New Light. They would name them things like that so it reflected their newfound faith.

He was such a humble man. Very competent. A thinker. Very detail oriented – between he and his wife in making sure the translation was accurate and all the diacritics. For the people to learn the language and read it, it is in Roman script. So that was helpful. They lived such an austere life. I don't know if they ever lacked the financial support because they lived such a simple lifestyle. Always, even to this day, the house that they lived in, in Waxhaw, is very basic. I think George, after Helen died, lost some weight because food wasn't a priority – just to live – and that was the way he looked at it. He was always thin, because food wasn't a priority with him.

Probably [we prayed most about] some of the Spiritual challenges among the people. I remember the days when they were setting up the infrastructure of the church that was coming along, and training the elders, and bringing other missions into this so there'd be a partnership among the missions. Then, of course, there was always revenge kinds of things that would happen – "so-and-so hurt me, and so I'm going to harm his family, or kill somebody".

That would happen out there. Not as much as the other groups, but there was some revenge kinds of things from time to time. I never heard of it greatly; I heard of some incidents with a machete where they cut each other pretty badly. I never heard of an incident where they used their shotguns to go after someone. I know at one point, there was a guy – he was not one of them, but he knew the language and he was taking advantage of him financially, and one day he just disappeared. Jim Daggett told me about that one, and he said "Two or three guys went on a trip with him, and the three guys arrived alone." So, who knows what happened.

[Their religion was] animistic – the spirits – the spirit world. I have often theorized, with most of the groups they believed in the spirit world, but they were all bad. They always had to appease them. They always had to sacrifice an animal or do something to make the spirits happy. So suddenly, when they heard about the Good Spirit of God, it was easy. This was something they'd been looking for, for years, so this was something easy for them to get into and accept.

Sandy: And the good news [for them] is that the Good Spirit is stronger than any of those other spirits.

Butch: And a question you might want to ask of someone who lived there and worked with them is: "Was there ever a confrontation between the powers of darkness and the powers of light, and what did that look like?" because those almost always happened. When the Scripture came in and the people started reading and started applying that, then the witchdoctors would come up and would challenge that power and authority. And a lot of witchdoctors came to the Lord, because they realized that they didn't have the power that this other Power was. Now, I don't know of any specific stories among the Chayahuitas, but I would venture to say that they're there.

Sandy: Speaking of what we would pray about, I just remember there were some young Chayahuita men that they were thinking would help them with the translation and so forth, and some of them – they thought they'd made a commitment to Christ – and then they'd wander away and go back into their old ways. I just remember Helen and George just being brokenhearted, like if it was their own kids!

Butch: Probably, the greatest temptation in a group like that is alcohol. Traders would bring in the different kinds of whiskeys. Immorality was always a problem, because they didn't have a specific system: everybody knew who everybody's wife was, but sometimes, they strayed away from that, and so there was immorality and those kinds of things. Those things happened, which caused a lot of anger and strife in the tribe.

He was more or less a trainer. Now, there was another mission near us that we called the Swiss. It was a Swiss-Indian mission, "Peruvianized." They would do some basic training of the men, and then they would take them to the Swiss mission for specific Scriptural training on how to lead a Bible study, and more Scriptural knowledge. As pilots, we'd bring them in for four months at a time. And they'd be at that course, studying, and then they'd go back and, generally, be the pastor. But they'd have to keep working, they'd have to keep their fields, because if they don't keep their fields, the crop doesn't come in and they don't eat. It's as simple as that. Hunting; fishing –

happens all the time. They live day to day. They used to have bows and arrows and blowguns, not they had shotguns. 16 gauge shotgun was the standard government issue.

Sandy: [George] discipled one-on-one these young men and women who would help him in translation, but intentionally did not put himself in the role of pastor.

Butch: In his work with them in the translation process, he'd work with one or two people and then, to check a passage of Scripture, they would get a committee of people and they would read back to them what they had translated; what it meant. Sort of like a naïve translation check. And they'd ask them: "What'd this say to you?" And they'd ask key questions to see if the meaning came through or not. I know in the highlands among the Quechua, they translated the Christmas story. One guy took it up and read the story to two people. Before his day was over, there was a crowd and he'd read it seven or eight times. And he'd get the comment: "I've never heard a story like this before. Never in my language." So it spoke.

Of course, they'd make corrections in grammar and some

of those kinds of things and can you say it better another way, but some of the groups had problems. Now, this wasn't the Chayahuita, but some of them didn't know what a rock was. There are no rocks on the central jungle. Now, they're more in the foothills, so there's all kinds of rocks. But, you know when they translated that passage: "Upon this rock, I will build my church." Some of the groups don't know what that is. So, they would use an ironwood – that would be the center-pole of all of their houses. "Upon this center-pole I will build my church." Well, the meaning is the same – it's the strength – it's not talking about a literal rock or a literal center-pole, its talking about the symbol that thing is to them. So all those kinds of things had to be faced in the translation process.

Sandy: [George] was always loving, but he was always serious. He was so focused on what he needed to do to get it done; there wasn't a whole lot of frivolity in his life. Nor Helen. I don't remember him not having a good time, but standing apart from others that I knew down there, he was very seriously focused.

Butch: Three years ago, he told me, he said: "You know,

I've got this amount of the project to finish, and when I finish that, I will have finished God's calling on my life." I can hardly repeat it, because most of us can't say that. But he stayed so focused and so committed.

You talk about committed! Commitment's another word I think of when I think of George and Helen. Commitment to this – this was their lifelong project.

Sandy: We were in a Covenant Group with him in recent years while Helen was still alive – past ten years say. The guys would take turns leading, and we'd be going through a certain Scripture and we were always looking forward to the times George did it, because he would start talking about when he translated this and the process he went through to make the people understand what it needed to say. And it was so good.

Butch: In a lot of those people groups, who your ancestors were was extremely important.

Sandy: I don't remember which country this was – it might have been Papua New Guinea – they almost just decided to skip the first part of Matthew, but they decided: "No, this is the whole Word of God." And that was the turning point for those people. "So that's who Jesus was! Man, he had all that lineage behind him!" And that made all the difference. They were glad they didn't skip over that.

Butch: A lot of them get back into ancestor worship. That's a part of who they have been. And then a big question that you often get is: "How long have you had the Gospel? How about your father and your grandfather?" Then it gets quiet…. "What took you so long?"

10

HE IS FOLLOWING WELL

"A friend loves at all times, and a brother is born for adversity."

– Proverbs 17:17 (NKJV)

I also had the opportunity to interview Jim and Carole Daggett in their home in Dallas, Texas. They showed me great hospitality and many thanks are due them for their generosity and willingness to tell me of their work with the Chayahuita. Jim and Carole worked closely with George and Helen for many years and got to know them well. They aided in translation, medical care, and maintenance of the aircraft used in the area among many other duties. The next many pages are devoted to their recollections.

We first met in 1968 when I was teaching but we started working with him as a team since 1971 when we were assigned to be a second team with George and Helen.

What they did in Peru at that time the administration would assign new people coming in and the members would have some choice in the matter, but in our case, we just asked the administration to assign us to the team where they thought we would fit best and where the need was greatest. And they said, "Well, George and Helen Hart really have a great need and they've been praying for a second team to come alongside and help out," so right away, we started working with them after we finished our Spanish study and some other things we had to do to be cleared for that assignment.

The first thing we did when we went out with the Chayahuita people: George and Helen had given us some basic lessons in Chayahuita grammar and some basic lessons that we could study. We didn't know very much when we got out there. Our first six weeks out there, George and I went out on a survey trip together and the women went back to our center at Yarinacocha. Our trip was to survey villages where George had never visited before. If you can imagine, the mountains were to the west and the jungle to the east and there was a main river that came down from the mountains and all these little tributaries. Well, George had been down the main river and partway up each of the other rivers. That's where I really started to get to know George, when we were out there together – these two men going from one river system to the next doing that survey – hiking and carrying our stuff, from one village to the next and meeting people.

At the time [the Chayahuita were] around 8,000 people but currently maybe 12,000 located up in the northern jungle area of the Amazon basin in northern Peru.

George and Helen and some others had classified the language earlier and its actually kind of isolated; it's not part of a family so much and there's only one other language group that's in the same family of languages and that group has pretty well died out and pretty much assimilated into Spanish. There are at least 12 different language families in Peru and over 60 languages, but Chayahuita is isolated. They have some long words from the highland people. Their number system – one to five – is their own, but when you go higher, they borrow from Quechua. It's a very live language and a very rich language.

I'm not a real whiz with languages so it was interesting. Carol was more the book person and I would go out and mix with the people. I'd come back in the house and say, "Now, Carol, there's something going on there and I don't quite understand the right grammar there." She would help me put it together and I would gather all the vocabulary because I was out with the people, so I was ahead of her in vocabulary, but she would help me put it together with the grammar. 'Course, when we with the Harts, they would help us too.

The neat thing about Chayahuita is that we learned to read it very early on, so I could read Chayahuita fluently, sometimes not even knowing exactly what I was reading by the patterns, so when you'd read it, you'd find it very easy to read. There weren't any real strange things going on. Some of the groups in Peru had tonal languages that were very complicated. The only feature that was a little distinctive in Chayahuita was a glottal stop. Like, p-a-a, if they put in the glottal, would be pa'a (pah-ah). There were some aspiration things that went in sometimes that were kind of features more for emphasis. It wasn't an extremely complicated language, but the grammar, you could do a lot with that language; it was a very rich language. They only had three vowels and seventeen letters in their alphabet.

That's what George and Helen did (transcribe the oral language into written). We came along after some time. They had done the linguistics and Carol and I just picked up more of the language.

The Chayahuitas lived on two different river systems and George and Helen liked to visit the people on both river systems and encourage the churches and the believers along there and it was just an impossible task for one family, so we could do what we called "Scripture use" following up with the church and the people that way. Some summers, when the kids were out of school, they'd go on one stretch and Carol and I would go on the other and we'd maybe switch river systems back and forth. Because the mountains were there on the east, like I said, and the one main river went down into the Matanyon which is one of the main tributaries of the Amazon. And the other one went down to the Huallaga, which was a little more to the south and came into the Ucayali River which later joins to form the Amazon with the Marañon.

We were fully active for about ten years, but later they asked me to be administrator I was over all programs jungle and highlands, but later we split that up because there were too many people working up in the highlands so we had a jungle administrator and a highland administrator. But even when I was in administration, I maintained contact with the Chayahuitas. I would get out there occasionally; we didn't go out as a family any more, but I would still go out and see them mainly for government officials. We were prayer partners with them right up until the end when we left in '94, and we still prayed for the Chayahuita people.

[George Hart] is a very modest man, athletic. He has a Master's degree in anthropology from Wheaton College. But he's so modest, he just doesn't toot his own horn at all so you can easily underestimate George Hart. He and Helen both liked to keep a low profile. They didn't want anyone talking about them very much. They're both very capable, but George is the kind of guy that until I got to know him, I didn't realize what a fantastic sense of humor he had! He had these wonderful stories he would tell me; they were just fascinating. I was just fortunate, I don't know of anyone else who had the opportunity to hear those stories like I did, because I was with him. His WWII stories: flying in a cargo plane over the Hump; barely having enough altitude to get over the highest mountains. He told about at least one close call. He was co-pilot, and the pilot dialed in the wrong frequency – they used a radio station as their guide – and there were two frequencies close together and they were headed right towards this mountain when George caught it. They just missed it, but barely!

Then he would tell stories about the Chayahuitas, in the early years; how difficult it was; how the people just wouldn't respond in any way to them. He said that the breakthrough really came when there was an outbreak of the eye infection that the kids get especially and they had tetracycline ointment and that was the first time that the people would allow any medical treatment at all. They depended completely on their shaman for their medical stuff. That opened the door a little bit. They were in a village called Solidad where there were a couple of believers but not much of a response to the Gospel and a village two days' walk away heard about this guy over there who was translating God's Word and they sent a delegation over – this was just before George and Helen were going to go on furlough. They listened to George talking there in Solidad and they invited him to come over to their village two days' walk away. He went over and they got all the people together there and listened. George said later they told him as they met they wondered: "Now, is he a deceiver? Is he deceiving us or is this really a good message? Is this God's Word; is he speaking the truth?"

He said that the women carried the day; they said, "Yes, we really believe that he has God's words for us." George and Helen were ready to leave on furlough and George said, "If you can build an airstrip here, when we come back from furlough, we'll come visit you." They did it! 'Course, they had to go check out the airstrip before they could go in there, but it passed muster and they went in. That village actually became the center of evangelism for the Chayahuitas. Those people really took God's Word to heart and not only their village, but they shared it and they sent missionaries out to other villages. There were some other villages later that responded in other ways, but they really reached out to a lot of people, and it was so encouraging to George and Helen to have that response from that village.

On that first trip with George, Carole and I were in a village called Nueva Vita. George flew out to another village called Balsa Puerto; they flew me out to be with George and that's where we started the survey trip. At Balsa Puerto, one of the Chayahuita had married a girl from some distance away and he came with a tape recorder of George reading the Scriptures on tape. Just with that – we had about an hour walk from where we were staying to Balsa Puerto – we came in on a Sunday morning and there were a hundred people gathered around the tape recorder listening to George's voice and here we walked in. It was just amazing the response of those people: here was a man who had been talking and we met with them.

There was another village we were wanting to go visit, and

every one of those villages, we would go up to the river and this was the last village we were on the "Salt" River or Cachiagu... it translates to "salt". I remember walking behind George and a couple of the Chayahuita men. We came to a cliff and the river was down below and there were little notches cut in the side of the cliff and we had to walk across – it was about fifty feet down below and we had to walk along the edge of that cliff. It was a good trail, but I remember for me that was quite an experience. We got up to that village upriver.

This was the pattern we followed on that survey: during the day, we would go up to the houses to visit; just let people know who we were, and we would invite them to come to an agreed upon home to hear God's Word that night.

Well, that village – I think there were like twelve or thirteen rapids that you had to go up in your canoe if you went by river – and I think it was because of that, those men; they were just big, burly...they were the biggest Chayahuita men I ever saw, really muscular strong guys...so we got together that first night—dark – a little tin can with a wick with kerosene; that was a light. All of us sitting around the men usually in the first circle and the ladies in the back circle and George started reading the Scripture. 'Course he knew the language, I wasn't in at all of what he was reading. And so he starts reading, and as he's reading it, these men were sitting there with their arms folded, sitting on these little chairs or stools that they would sit on and they would say: "Teyowonjachi, teyowonjachi ishapaya!" [deep, stern, guttural sounding] like that, you know, and George kept reading and they kept responding like that all the way through.

So afterwards, at night when we were all getting ready for bed, I said, "George, what was that 'teyowonjachi' thing? They were really shouting that out; it kinda scared me!"

He said: "That's kinda like, 'Amen!' 'That's true, brother!' It's an affirmation; they're saying, 'Yes, that's true!'"

Now, of course, today there's a strong church up there in Balsa Puerto and some really strong believers. That was memorable to me, those very first experiences with George and those experiences like that.

We didn't have the whole New Testament then. At the time, I was so green, I didn't know what he was reading, but he would usually take a recently translated book and read. It wasn't preaching; it was reading God's Word and maybe just amplifying it a little bit – explaining. The way he taught me to do it, what I kinda developed and what he reinforced was to read it and almost just repeat the key phrases and not get far from the Word of God; just let the Word of God speak and they were very effective.

Going on, then to the next river system, I think it was the very next river system we had to walk up over this mountain -- I don't know, maybe 5,000 feet or so – and I remember going uphill I was kinda puffing and I wasn't in the greatest shape and of course George is at least fifteen years older than me, maybe more and he said: "Jim, I don't mind going up these hills, but going down bothers my knee a bit!" That really bothered me, 'cause I was huffing and puffing to get up the hill and he was just charging away!

We got to the next village over and people fled. We had two Chayahuita men with us helping us carry some of our gear, and the Chayahuita guys went to the edge of the village and called out to the people and told them: "These people won't harm you!"

They brought the people back in and George overheard one o the ladies say, "We thought those white men had come to eat us!" They were really afraid of us.

But we began there and we shared and we went on up to the last house on that river and then downriver to the last house that he had been to coming from the main river so we could make the connection. In some of the very uppermost places on those rivers we did run into some who spoke the Highland Quechua, the San Martin Quechua, which is a neighboring group. In fact, in one home, there were like, four different languages going on: the Quechua and our English, the Chayahuita and then Spanish – it was kind of a mix in that place!

[Chayahuita and Quechua are very different] There's just a few lone words and the number system; otherwise they're not related at all.

I believe there was a movement there at Wheaton College.

I assume that was it. I know he and his brother Ray were both called to Wycliffe. I assume they were both from a strong church that had a strong missionary emphasis there in Michigan; that's where he grew up. That was during the time when Jim Elliot – you know, the martyrs – had taken place and these WWII veterans, a lot of them, really some Godly people came into missions organizations like The Navigators, really had an impact on the lives of some of those men. Anyway, I can't say exactly what it was that called George to it, except that he did it out of obedience to what the Lord was calling him to do.

George was so far ahead of me, and when we went together, it was pretty much in those early years. Later on, Carole and I would go out separately, we weren't going out as a team. They would go to one part of the tribe and we would go to the other.

There is kind of a cute story that happened. We were in a village one time and our girls – we have three daughters, but when we were there, there were just two daughters. In that village, we had a house that was on a platform, thatched roof, and we slept on the floor with mosquito nets, and out girls each had their own mosquito net. So one night I woke up, and here was a porcupine had gotten into our house. Just kind of the jungle version of a porcupine, a little different than what we have up here, and it was panicky, it was just dashing around and here my girls were. And I tried to get it out of the house, but I just couldn't the thing was just too agitated. So I grabbed the machete and just whacked it on the head and threw it out on the dirt in front of our house. It was the middle of the night. Well, in the morning I got up and here's this circle of people from the village, men and women and kids all in a big circle out there, looking down at porcupine. So, I made my little speech, you know, out there on the platform, and I went out there and I said: "Well, you know, I saved my children from an awful experience; it could have really hurt my kids, and so I…" And they all just nodded. Well, it turned out that about six weeks later, George went through that same village and he said he was sitting there – I found this out twenty years later, what had really happened there. And he said he had sat down and this guy came and sat down next to him. They had this small talk for a while, and then there was a pause. George said, "When there's that pause, you know the main topic is coming up." And so the man said to George, "You know, brother Jim was here a few weeks ago." George says, "Yeah, I know." The man says, "Well, I used to have a pet porcupine…" What was so funny about that; what makes it even funnier, was that here we were, we were having some kind of anniversary for George and Helen, and so I was going to be the MC for that and I said, "George, can you think of some humorous incident you can share with everyone at the get-together, and he told that story, and that's the first time I heard that! "I used to have a pet porcupine…" Who would have a pet porcupine, for one thing! What a pet!

George had a way, with just a slight smile on his face, he could really tell a story beautifully.

It's funny, because the next morning, we had a generator at Yarinacocha, and the guys who maintained that went in, and there's a porcupine in the generator room! They'd never seen one in there, so they put it in a laundry basket, and took it over and put it in my office, just as kind of a joke, a follow-up to that story, and that made it even funnier!

I really feel like the Chayahuita church, the group, has really been one of the more responsive of the language groups in Peru. There are a lot of really good responses to different language groups. Some of them there, I was part of a study group that came from the Untied States to see how evangelism was going in Peru. It was part of a movement and they wanted everyone in the world to be sure to hear the Gospel presented clearly. They were doing that for the jungle area of Peru. So I was in these meetings, and they would get these men together from different groups and they would say, "Now, we'd like to help you begin to develop a strategy so that everyone in your language group hears the Gospel clearly presented." Well, I don't know how many of them said, "We've already done that; it's already been done! We've seen to it that everybody has an opportunity to know Christ and knows clearly." And that was some of the larger groups too, and others were moving in that direction.

Among the Chayahuitas, even though George and Helen are gone, the Word of God is having this brilliant impact.

Now, there's a missionary there; one of his ministries is soccer and the Chayahuitas love soccer. So, they had this invitation for everyone to come into one of the larger villages and for everyone to have a soccer tournament. Well, people were coming in from villages we never knew existed to play soccer! And they all heard the Gospel message, so it's an ongoing thing; so you have God's Word in their language now.

Basically, when we were in Intervarsity, Carole and I went to the Urbana missions conference. At that time, we filled out a little card that said, "We don't feel called to missions now but we're open." So that was kind of an understanding that we had; that if the Lord really called us to the mission field, that we'd do that. Carole's folks had gone on a long-term trip to Africa, and had come back really excited about mission work and the opportunities there. Then at Urbana, we had that experience, and then when I was teaching school, I was teaching a Sunday school class in our church, and Carole was in an adult class, and a missionary from Wycliffe spoke and he said, "We really need a teacher." This was in April. He said,

"My daughter's in sixth grade and she's not going to have a teacher this year; they're going to have to take a translator in from their translation work because there's just no teacher showing up. So pray about a teacher." Well, Carole came home and told me all about it. So we called the missionary up and – wonderful man, Dan Bailey, his name is – Dan just walked us through the whole [process]. Back then, you didn't go to Wycliffe headquarters, you went to the administration out in the field; you got on the HAM radio (that was the only communication at the time). That was April, and in August, we were there. I resigned my teaching job for the short-term thing. We thought it would be for one year, then we saw that there was a place for us there; that we could really fit in. The Lord just led us along.

Right now, Carole is a personnel administrator for people who are on furlough or between assignments; so she works with all those people. My job, right now, is called "partnership development consultant" and it's a faith mission, so each missionary builds their team of partners and I'm just consulting with people all the time. We have workshops, I do a lot of face to face (today I had several telephone interviews). I meet with people just to help them along in there partnership development. A lot of our people in Wycliffe are introverts, and it's just not natural for them to reach out. They say you can tell an extroverted engineer because he looks at <u>your</u> feet when he talks to you. That's kind of the way it is with linguists and translators; they're the same way.

I've had different roles, I did what Carole's doing – personnel administration – for a while, when we got back. We used to have regional offices, and when we had regional offices, my job was in several different areas, but now it's just narrowed down to one. I'm almost seventy years old, so we're kind of cutting back; we're not quite as active as we were when we were your age!

Even when they came back, hey would still make trips down to work with the committee, and now with electronic communication the way it is, even though they were in Waxhaw, they still kept on top of things with the Chayahuita. There was a committee there working on an Old Testament translation and some revision of the New

Testament, so they've been on top of that ever since. George just made a trip within the last year, down again, but his health isn't so good now, so he had to come back, I think earlier than he anticipated. It would have been 1993 [that he moved back to Waxhaw].

When I was in college, a small town boy at the University of Minnesota, working nights to get my way through school, and way over my head in the academics! I was a very sloppy high school student, so it was a struggle for me. And being a Christian, but not a very mature Christian at that time, I felt that there was something really missing. I remember going to church one Sunday night and the pastor gave a message that really touched me, and I went home and just started reading the Scriptures, especially the book of James just came out to me, like it was the Lord speaking to me, just to me personally. I remember praying at that time for fellowship; I was working at that time about forty-eight hours, most of the year we were working six nights a week. Even to meet a girl was …[difficult]. To have a ministry fellowship and a relationship, and I think it was within a week someone invited me to the Intervarsity chapter meeting, and very soon I was leading a Bible study and had fellowship with these other people, 'cause like I said, during the noontime where I could get in on it. Then later, I met Carole there, so it was just pretty amazing.

I think if you talk to most Bible translators who are in Wycliffe, they'll say – you know the question you asked just now – they'll say that it was "because God's Word spoke to me personally and I know how powerful it is, and I want it to be available to people who don't have it yet." When I first was out there and couldn't really speak the language at all, but could read it, one night they called me – no, it wasn't at night, it was during the daytime – they said, "Just downriver, there's a man named Shanti who's been a shaman, a witchdoctor, and he's been taking these hallucinatory drugs and all, and he's dying, and he wants you to come an tell him how he can go to heaven."

So, Carole and I got out the passage – there were just little booklets of Scripture we had available at the time – we just mapped out the Scripture verses that I could read to him that would give him the plan of salvation, just what he needed to do it. So I went down there with one of the men to where this guy was laying in his hammock there pretty sick and talked to him in the baby-talk that I was speaking at the time and then started to read the Scriptures that Carole and I had selected. I just read one of them and the next one and the next one and after a while I realized that he was weeping, the guy was just – big strong man, one of the biggest Chayahuitas you'll ever see. And then I asked him if he wanted to pray and receive Christ as his Savior. Oh, he prayed a beautiful prayer! So afterwards I went back and I told George about it, and he said, "Well, Jim, those shaman are so powerful , and it's really hard for them to give up their practices, so don't be surprised if…"

But, I would go back to that area and ask, "How is Shanti doing?" "Oh, he's following well!" they'd say, "He got better!"

I remember there was a snakebite case that was down in his neighborhood, and he went with me to treat the snakebite case, and he brought along lemons. And this woman who had been bit by the snake – I later read that Vitamin C is really a good thing for snakebite – so I was giving these injections of the anti-venom and he was ministering to her with the lemons and comforting her, but not with the old chants and all the other things they used to do, but really in an appropriate way. To me, it's just another example of how powerful God's Word is and how it spoke to him.

That big survey trip, and I think maybe there were just one or two trips where just George and I would go out together. We would have these conferences for Christian leadership and we would be involved together. They would be there right out in the villages, we would choose a village and do them right there. We had our center where we would have our prayer meetings together but the Chayahuitas was about a two and a half hour flight in a small place to get out to the villages.

Carole and I had a dugout canoe we would travel in to the villages on both river systems, so we'd get around that way. George and Helen didn't travel by river much, they pretty much went in by airplane to different villages

The elders' conferences for leadership, it was really neat the way that worked, it was interesting. The first

Chayahuita believers were baptized in the church; Jim Elliott's brother, Bert Elliott, was leading down in the market town, down at the mouth of the main river. Then, they were appointed as elders, then they were qualified then to baptize the people in their villages, they were trained. There was a Bible school near where our center was that specialized in training in Spanish some of the native pastors, so some of the Chayahuitas got that training too. That was another part of the leadership; that's been a pretty strong program there. It was a Swiss group of missionaries who kept that one going.

George liked to play tennis; we had a little cement tennis court there and he liked to talk about jogging. I'd go out when I was lighter than I am now, and I would jog for an hour; well George would come out and sprint around our little track – we had a soccer field and built the track around it – and he would run just two laps, but at a pretty fast speed. And he played some basketball, every year the high-schoolers would have their flag football season, and they needed a team to play against, so for several years I was the quarterback and George was the halfback – he's very fast. He was on the track team at Wheaton College. I remember practicing one day, and I was going to hand the ball off to George and we collided and my glasses got shattered when we bumped heads! Like I said, he was very athletic, he loved to play tennis, he played basketball for a long time, then moved upward to tennis after a while.

He was a good father and he loved his kids. One of the cute things we would see: he had a little dog called Four-eyes – the dog had its eyes, then it had two little markings that looked like two more eyes, so they named him Four-eyes. George would go around the center on this little Honda 90 (almost like a moped) and the little dog sitting on the seat right behind him. Going around together, that was kind of the...I don't know anyone else who would have that going for them where he had the dog riding around with him – a little rat terrier kind of dog.

He knew the Word. He and Helen were a real team in the translation; they worked very well together. Some of the other married couples you would see where one was maybe a lot stronger than the other in the linguistics or whatever was going on. In their case they were very much a team and they worked together very effectively.

The quiet strength that he had. He was so respected, he would be elected often to the executive committee which was the key committee for the administration of our work there in Peru. He was not one that would push himself forward and I really appreciated that. You would have to kind of draw him out in a group. He would listen and contribute, but not very often; he would tend to be on the quiet side. Helen would sometimes say, "Well, I wish George, what he said was so good, I wish he'd have said more!" He was very concise; a man of few words I guess you'd say. A lot of wisdom, I appreciated that, the wisdom that he had. I remember him telling me early on, he said, "Jim, the more I work with these people, the more I understand the passage that talks about the sower broadcasting the seed and how it falls: some of it falls on good ground as some of it doesn't, you know some of it lands on bad ground; some of it bears fruit and some doesn't." He had those Biblical principles really solid and that's what he based his life and his ministry on.

We'd understand and then George and Helen would

explain what's going on. We noticed at one point, when we'd see a couple that we hadn't seen for a while, sometimes they would stand before us and weep, just as we met them; it might even be an older couple. So, we asked George and Helen, "What's going on there?"

And they said, "That's customary in their society when they've lost somebody, like a young couple, when a baby has died, out of respect to that baby, the next time they see you, that's the appropriate thing to do; or if an adult loses a brother or sister.

George had said that there were some really cute things that would happen because the people were so naïve about things that were going on in the New Testament. One example they gave me was when they were translating the story about forgiving your enemies, that passage about forgiving your enemies. So they had the translators helping George and Helen. They thought they had it really good, you know, "Pray for your enemies." They often would check them with someone else who was hearing it for the first time, and they would call that person a native informant: someone who hadn't been through the whole process and knew the background. So, they found this guy

who was a native informant. And they read the passage,

and George said: "Now, what does that say?"

And the guy said, "Well, it says I should pray for my

enemies."

And George says, "And how would you pray?"

"I would pray that they would get sick and die!"
So then they had to tune it up a little bit so that you would

pray positively over something like that!

Another time they were translating the passage that says,

"A certain man had a hundred sheep…."

And the Chayahuitas heard that and they started laughing;

they were just cracking up! And George couldn't

understand why. It turned out they had been down to

Yurimaguas, the market town, and occasionally you'd see

someone with three or four sheep, but the idea of

someone with a hundred sheep was just ridiculous! "A

certain man had a hundred sheep!" No way! Somehow in

their sense of humor, it just really cracked them up!

Anyway, they had some interesting stories there with the

translation.

The Chayahuitas were such a sharing people. Some of these are stories that don't involve George, but they're kind of interesting. Well, I think this one is kind of an interesting cultural thing: Carole did a study over at the University of Oklahoma. She did a course of anthropology there, and she wrote a paper on Musato – it's a drink, kind of like a beer that the people, it's one of the staples of their diet, where they drink it, and Carole documented how it is so much a part of their culture. The women make a special skirt that they put out only to serve that musato, only on those occasions. And the serving bowl – beautiful – when they're done in the legitimate style of the culture of their people, they're really a work of art. And then, when a group of men are in a home, the wife will put on her special skirt over her other skirt, and she will come around to each man and serve the musato. She will serve her husband first and then the others. Well, George and I, on that survey trip, as we got closer and closer down the Yurimaguas, the market town, you could just see the Spanish culture's influence; where there was intermarriage sometimes things just got a little sloppier. Finally, we got to this one home and this woman gets up to serve the musato: she reaches up into the rafters and pulls out this yellow slip that she had bought in town, pulls that on over her head, grabs an aluminum bent up beat up bowl off the ground, and goes around and serves musato! And they just completely lost all the beauty of it, but they were just going through the motions. So you can just see how the beauty of how the Scriptures can come in and one of the effects of having the Word of God in their own language is that it gave prestige to the language to have it written and materials: schoolbooks, health books, everything that George and Helen had done translated into Chayahuita. So they didn't have to jump into this other society which in many ways wasn't as beautiful as their own. It just wasn't them.

The people wanted to grow beans, and so I thought I had the translation right of "beans," and so I went around and took orders from the villagers. And so, when the plane came, I had bean seed to pass out, and they accepted it, but then they said, "But, where's the corn?" And I had got the words mixed up! They were happy for the beans, but I had used corn all the way through and so they wanted corn seed!

He loved those little stories of the people; some of the daily events that went on there. They had one – talking about that musato – George and Helen were on a flight with one of the Chayahuita people and the guy was coming in for some training at the center. And his mother had packed this musato: they make it into a kind of a mass, you know, a paste, but very dehydrated, so it's still moist, but to reconstitute it, you have to add a lot of water to it. To transport it, you just make it into a big ball and wrap it in banana leaves. So, she's got it all wrapped up and they're on the plane, George and Helen, with this Chayahuita guy, and they're up at about 18,000 feet in altitude. All of a sudden there's this terrible explosion, and they're wondering, what in the world! And all of them were just splattered with this stuff, and that fermented stuff in the altitude had made this stuff just – Poofff! And it made quite a sound, besides splattering everybody with musato; the whole inside of the plane, all the passengers and the pilot were covered; George told that story.

Another story he told me was when they first went to
Peru, the flight from Lima on Pacific was over the Andes
out to the jungle in a DC-3, and the DC-3 did not have the
ceiling that would get you over the mountains, you had to
go through this one pass. And Helen didn't like to fly; she
was not comfortable with flying. George said that one
time they were flying through the pass and he looked out
the window and one of the engines had stopped. They
were feathering one engine, and he said, "I didn't have the
heart to tell Helen." They made it, but, obviously, not
with a lot to spare. He, being a former pilot, he knew what
was going on.

They were quite a pair, George and Helen. She was a
doctor's daughter, she grew up in Chattanooga, in a very
comfortable area, and for Helen, it was a step down to
move out to those little huts in the village.

Here's another example of what it was like for them: the
people were just so curious about our style of living, and
Helen would just about go crazy for lack of privacy. The
kept making their houses smaller and smaller to try and get

more privacy, so people couldn't be coming in and all on top of them! Finally, they had the house about as small as it could get. And they put in this, it's called "pona", it's palm bark or palm tree and these slats are maybe three inches wide and those form your walls, and they're tied together with vines around the house. And then they had a little table with a window so they could look out to the jungle in Solidad where they had this one house. Well, first of all, they cut off the flooring, which is another kind of flooring that you spread out; you chop down a palm tree and spread it out, and that becomes almost as wide, and you lay those out kind of like a springboard. So, you do have a floor. And here's the wall with the slats, and then they tried to get the guys to cut them off right at the edge so people couldn't stand outside their window on the edge and look in at them! But, it didn't work. Even with just an inch or so, they are barefooted, and they knew how to just dig their toes in and so they'd be sitting there eating and here'd be this row of faces looking at them. They just couldn't seem to convince people – well, people would come from miles away to see these outsiders, so maybe in the village itself, they'd have people educated, but there

was always someone coming in. Then George finally put
these poles out from in front, so that would dissuade
people from coming and he had the poles installed. So,
they sat down to eat; a guy comes in and lies down on the
pole and is watching them – that just about drove Helen
completely out of her head! This guy thinks that they've
provided a bed for them, so that he can recline and watch
them! Anyway, they had their times there! Helen was kind
of high-strung; George was calm and even, but she was a
nervous type, but she was a wonderful translator and
linguist, and they were a neat couple.

I mentioned the music among the Chayahuitas, and that
was probably one of the most effective parts of the
ministry with the Chayahuitas. They had not had much of
a tradition of music among themselves. They had flute
and drum dance music at their festival occasions, where
they would often get drunk and dance and play their flute
and drums, but they didn't have songs that they would sing
at all: maybe a few little lullabies the mothers would kind
of hum to the babies, but Helen especially really got going
on the music and there was a regional music with the

Quechua people and so they borrowed from the Quechuas a lot of the tunes that were really beautiful tunes. With each of the choruses or songs, they would have a Scripture verse, so the people would wing when they had their meetings, they would all sing together and recite the verse. So, they were memorizing Scripture right along with the songs that they were singing.

I remember how beautiful it was to go through the village and hear these children singing these choruses, these Christian songs, where earlier, they hadn't had anything like that, so the music really was a big deal. Later, some of them learned to play guitar and they got their own music groups going and so there was jus a lot of joy in the music. And it was just beautiful to see that.

Then, I wanted to tell you about something that's very meaningful to me. When Carole and I first went out into the villages, you could walk into any house, it seemed like every house – there were a few exceptions. The people usually had a dirt floor or just a very simple bark kind of a flooring, but most often it was a dirt floor. And the place where they stored their most important items was in the thatch – up in the thatch of the roof. And I noticed that in that place there'd usually be a machete or two there, a bull-gun and a 16-gauge Stevens shotgun. Those items were all potential weapons of warfare – the machetes they'd use for their gardens and stuff, and the bull-gun mostly for small animals and birds, although with the poison dart they could kill larger animals, and of course the shotgun for the tapir and the wild pigs and all. So that was always there: the shotgun, the machete, and the bull-gun. Well, during my last trip there in 1994, I noticed as I went from house to house, the machete, the bull-gun and the shotgun were still there, but now there was a New Testament and a hymnal; and those weapons of warfare were joined by Spiritual weapons of warfare. So, I noticed in the mornings the father would take the New Testament and the hymnal and would get his family together and they would have their family devotions together. In some villages, they would have a morning service and/or an evening service and you'd see them get down the New Testament and the hymnal and walk to the service. Just the beauty of seeing God's Word joining those other important artifacts there, were in the village and in the homes.

We went out to one of the villages, a very isolated village; it was a village out in the middle of nowhere. The pilots always depended on the rivers for their navigation – that was before any kind of GPS or anything – but this village was out where there was just a little tiny creek that went through there, and they didn't have any kind of landmarks to go by. They would use compass headings to try and find the village: I know one time we had our radio contact with our center and the pilot came on and said, "Tell me when you can hear me, because I can't find you guys!" We were down in that village, and finally, we heard that engine and said, "You're south of us, come north." And he eventually found us. In that village, we came out with a newly translated book of 1st John, and at the first site, we were there, the people asked us to share, and I took 1st John up and for the first time they were hearing these words: "Iwatarotsa isuciricaapantagama ico iwacapitantama ta isi gantoma wa hae. Quisochristo mantanatone ..."

And I just read the first part of that, and you know those verses, the way they come across is: "I was with Christ; I was with Jesus, and I saw Him, I heard Him, I touched Him, and now I'm writing this so you can know Him just as I did. So you can share the joy...." is the way it comes through "share my joy". But that came across to the people and you could just feel it in the air, and afterwards, sometimes people weren't too excited about getting copies of the Scriptures, you know there'd be a few who... but everyone wanted a copy of that because it is just so powerful and when you think of it, it's just a very beautiful passage to be able tot tell people for the first time: "Now you can know Him, just as I did because I'm writing it down!" That's 1st John 1:1-4.

[Of the verses read to the shaman] I'm sure John 3:16 was in there, some passages from Romans that just clearly explain our condition and how we can know Christ through faith. Probably a mix from the epistles that we had from the Gospels.

[The Chayahuita] had a lot of monkeys, a couple varieties of wild pig, some beautiful birds: the toucan, some that were kind of related to the partridge, that kind of a larger bird. Good fishing, they had a lot of fish in their diet. On of their customs was to collect the root of a plant called the barbasco plant, and then the night before a big fishing party, you'd hear them beating on the rocks, beating up that barbasco root into a pulp. Then, they'd go down to a stream and they'd block off one end of the stream, and they'd add water to the barbasco pulp, and it'd make the fish come to the suface. And there'd be this big event where the people would be collecting these fish. I remember one time we were on it and our daughter Joni was maybe three years old, and she noticed that to kill a fish, the people would put the fish head in their mouth and bite on the fish to kill the fish. Well, little Joni grabbed a fish and bit the head right off! So a lot of the people got a big kick out of that, that she bit the head off the fish instead of just biting it hard enough to kill it!

The tapir was the biggest of the jungle animals. There were jaguars; I never saw one but there was a certain variety of bear that lived just up in the slightly higher elevations. Unfortunately, especially with the introduction of the shotgun, the wild game population was falling off and the people were depending more and more on – they had chickens – they had to depend on other sources rather than just the wild meat. The men would go out on hunting trips for three or four days at a time, and they'd have to go a long ways back into the jungle to find the wild game. And it could be dangerous. The wild pigs traveled in herds, I guess you'd call them; they could kill you if they got after you and surrounded you. There's a story: one of the men got cornered, and with a single shotgun you can't do much, and usually you had only three or four shells anyway. His choice was to either stand there and get attacked by the pigs or climb up a prickly palm tree that have these thorns about this long [here Jim gestured something several inches in length], and so he had to climb the tree to get away from the pigs. He had a lot of thorns to pull out of himself after he finished up! And I got hit with those thorns in the back of my hand one time, and not only does it hurt, but there's something in there that makes it hurt even worse.

We ate a lot of different kinds of animals there with them: the mahas [also known as a paca], which is in the rodent family, but big, much bigger – it would be similar to a nutria that they have in Louisiana, if you've ever seen a picture of a nutria, it's a pretty big sized animal, but it's even bigger than a nutria.

There were always the rats. There was one kind of a cute story where Carole got up in the night with the kids, and we were in the village there, and of course the people can hear everything that's going on, you know, the houses are all open. And a mouse went scooting across the floor and Carole screamed and the next day the people were asking about what happened last night. And Carole said she saw a mouse. So, a little while after that I went with a couple of men who invited me to go to another village, on an evangelism trip – Pancho and Descente – so, we got over to the other village, and the first night we were sleeping in this house. And all of a sudden, Descente lets out a squawk, and it turns out a mouse had gotten up by his nose or something. And Pancho said: "Carolina bochin." "Like Carole." And they started laughing, and they couldn't control themselves because Descente had reacted just like Carole had with the mouse! Yeah, we had our little stories too!

The trails were hard for me because I weighed over 200 pounds and every time there was a little ravine, the people would put in a little bridge which is basically a four-inch diameter pole, and these are people who weigh maybe a hundred and twenty or thirty pounds and they could just go right across, barefooted. They'd go scooting across and here I was with my boots on and being so heavy; on that same trip with Pancho and Descente, when we were over at the other place, I came down with malaria. On the way over, instead of trying to cross those little bridges – and they seemed like they would come up all the time, and I would walk down to the bottom and then up, rather that try to cross over. Well, on the way back, here I was so weak from the malaria, I could barely move. So these guys had me, one on each elbow kind of helping me along. And each time we came to a ravine, they would make guard rails across it – they would take their machetes, and cut poles and make a bridge. And they had another four-inch or bigger log across. I t took us a long time to get back, I think it took about twelve hours, but they just stood with me all the way, making little bridges all the way, and it was really beautiful the way they took care of me.

That trip I made with George – George was much smaller and he could do it, and then I had high lace-up boots for the snakes) and George just had short boots, and he could get his off and on real quick if we had to wad e through a river or something. He was forever getting way ahead of me and I would be trying to catch up, after getting my boots back on every time! But the trails: it was amazing; I followed people through those trails, and I wondered how do they know where they're going? And I remember, on that same trip, Descente, as we got into an area where there'd be a fork in the road, he'd look up at the sun, and he'd go like that [gesture] and calculate, and then take the right trail.

This fellow who just died this week, when we first started, I remember he told me: "Jim, never go anywhere without a machete or without one of the Chayahuita men if you're going on trips." And boy, that paid off more times… I think the best example was when we had our little family, and we had a guy named Eloi with us – his Chayahuita name was Yrkin -- and we came around this little bend in a pretty shallow river, it wasn't much of a river. And here was a huge tree that had fallen across the river. Here we are with a twenty five foot canoe, we've got all of our stuff and this Briggs and Stratton engine with the long tail on it. How are we going to get over? Eloi took his machete and went off into the jungle, and we heard him chopping back there, and he came back with a big slab of bark. And he put it with the rough side down on top of the log. The inside was slimy, just like grease, just a real slimy slippery... We unloaded the canoe, put everything on the other side of the log, and then he said, "Now, you get back there with that motor, and sit way at the back so the nose of the canoe is up high, and go full speed at that slab of bark." So I did, and we got up there, about halfway – almost halfway, not quite halfway over – and then we were able to take the motor off, and pushed everything over the rest of the way and moved everything and went on our way. I would have never known how to do that, but with one of the locals there, we made it!

Mark Sirag, Bert Elliot, Arbito (a Chayahuita), George Hart
c. 1970

11

LABOR AND REST

Then I heard a voice from heaven say, "Write this: Blessed are the dead

who die in the Lord from now on." "Yes," says the Spirit, "they will rest

from their labor, for their deeds will follow them."

– Revelation 14:13

Life in Peru among the Chayahuita was not easy, but the Hart

family did not count it a hardship to be there or do the work that God gave

them to do. George and Helen returned to the United States during

furloughs and then in the 1980s, they made permanent residence in

Waxhaw, North Carolina.

The Lord called Helen home first. She passed away April 22, 2006

and George was no longer the same. He continued to be involved in

spreading the gospel and encouraging his brothers and sisters through

prayer and participation in a covenant group at Christ Covenant Church in

Matthews, North Carolina. There and at JAARS, many of his fellow laborers still gather and lift one another up in prayer and serve quietly as

examples of Godliness and Christ-like behavior to those around them.

George was not to remain in Waxhaw, however.

His health deteriorated, and his family felt it prudent to bring him

closer to them so that they could care for him better. He resided with them

for a time, until the difficulties that Alzheimer's disease brings made care

for him very difficult. His family obtained professional nursing care from a

home in Michigan. They continued to care for him, and he continued to

love them even when his memory failed to serve him to remind him of their

names or relation to himself. God called his faithful servant home on

August 30, 2012.

The final word of this biography I'll leave to the Daggett family:

Jim Daggett: Carole, could you think of a verse that
describes George, or more than one verse?

Carole Daggett: Jim, did you tell him about what the
Chayahuitas gave him at the dedication?

Jim: Yeah, that's a wonderful story. The Chayahuitas are
very stingy with their thank you's. They have ways of

expressing gratitude, but not verbally. Like, if we did

medical work and saved a child's life or something, they

would come and get the baby and take off. But then later

they'd maybe bring us some eggs or some wild meat or

something. To express gratitude was not often – you

didn't expect it from them, and anyway, if you did get

some eggs, that was unusual. When we, at the dedication

of the New Testament, we got everybody together in our

auditorium at Yarinacocha, and I was the master of

ceremonies. And I had lined up, we had some visitors

down from the United States and we were showing them

how the aviation department. School teachers had had a

part of this, and different things like that, and then of

course we were talking about George and Helen, how the

translation went. Well, up in the front row, on my left,

there was about six or more Chayahuitas from that Bible

school who had come over and I didn't know they were

coming and I didn't even have them on the program.

When we were maybe two-thirds of the way through the

program, they just came up to the front and they kind of

took over the meeting for a few minutes. They came, and

the women had made a scroll that they'd embroidered, and

they gave it to George and Helen, and they unrolled it and Helen just let out this little squeal!

And it said in Chayahuita: "Not in vain have you labored." [Tears fall as he relates this] 1st Corinthians 15:58 "Not in vain have you labored among us." Oh it was just one of the most amazing things I ever saw; it was just a beautiful story. And it was so sweet, so precious; that really meant a lot to me as you can tell.

Bibliography

Barkman, Butch and Sandy; (2009); Interview with Ian Smith…; cassette tape 1/1/09, Ian Smith's Library.

The Bible; (NIV Translation).

The Bible; (NKJV Translation).

Daggett, Jim and Carole; (2009); Interview with Ian Smith…; cassette tape 1/1/09, Ian Smith's Library.

Ethnologue; (2013); Online Version; *Chayahuita*; http://www.ethnologue.com/show_languages.asp?code=cbt

Hart, Doug; (2009); Dad Memories 4; sound file on disc "George Hart"; files copied to disc 11/29/09, Ian Smith's Library.

Isaacson, Ashley E., ed., et al.; (2005); <u>Let's Go: Peru</u>; St. Martin's Press.

McIntyre, Loren; (1975); <u>The Incredible Incas and their Timeless Land</u>; The National Geographic Society.

IAN SMITH

ABOUT THE AUTHOR

Ian Smith is a teacher and a servant and adopted son in the Christian family of God.

29601273R00074

Made in the USA
Middletown, DE
27 February 2016